My Little Blue Helmet

Abby Blackbu

Illustrations by Angel Dela

Order this book online at www.trafford.com
or email orders@trafford.com

Most Trafford titles are also available at major online book retailers.

Illustrations by Angel dela Pena.

Printed in the United States of America.

ISBN: 978-1-4669-7006-9 (sc)
ISBN: 978-1-4669-7007-6 (e)

Library of Congress Control Number: 2012924037

Trafford rev. 01/11/2013

www.trafford.com

North America & international
toll-free: 1 888 232 4444 (USA & Canada)
phone: 250 383 6864 • fax: 812 355 4082

For my son, Miller Blackburn, who inspired this book during his treatment for plagiocephaly.

Also to our sweet friends and family that encouraged us daily during our journey with Miller's helmet.

We dedicate this book to the Lord, who graciously carries us through every different season in life and brings us joy in the midst of trials.

MILLER

One night, Miller was in his room, getting ready for bed.

"Mama, will you tell me a story before I go to sleep?" Miller asked with a big yawn.

"Of course," replied Mama.

"What would you like to hear?"

"Tell me about my little blue helmet!"

"Again?" asked Mama as she picked up the photo album.

"Yes, again," said Miller.

"It all began when you were
a tiny baby."

"We noticed that
your head wasn't completely
round. Your doctor said you had
plagiocephaly, which is a big word
that means your head was flat
on one side."
"He recommended a special helmet
to help correct the shape of your head."

"To make my head round?" asked
Miller.

"That's right!"

"They fit you for the helmet and asked us to pick out a color."
"We chose **blue!**"
"We went for checkups every two weeks. They would measure your head and adjust the helmet each visit."

"Were you and Daddy sad that I had to wear the helmet?" asked Miller as he looked up at Mama.

"We were nervous and sad on that first day, but we very quickly fell in love with your little blue helmet," said Mama as she gave a wink.

"You were very handsome in your helmet."

"Did I wear the helmet
everywhere?"

"Yes, everywhere!"

"You wore it to the grocery store
and to restaurants. You wore it to church
and to day care. You wore it while you
were awake and asleep."

"You wore it to visit friends and family."
"You even wore it to the beach."
"You wore it everywhere!"

"Did people stare?" asked Miller.

"Sometimes they did, but they were just curious."

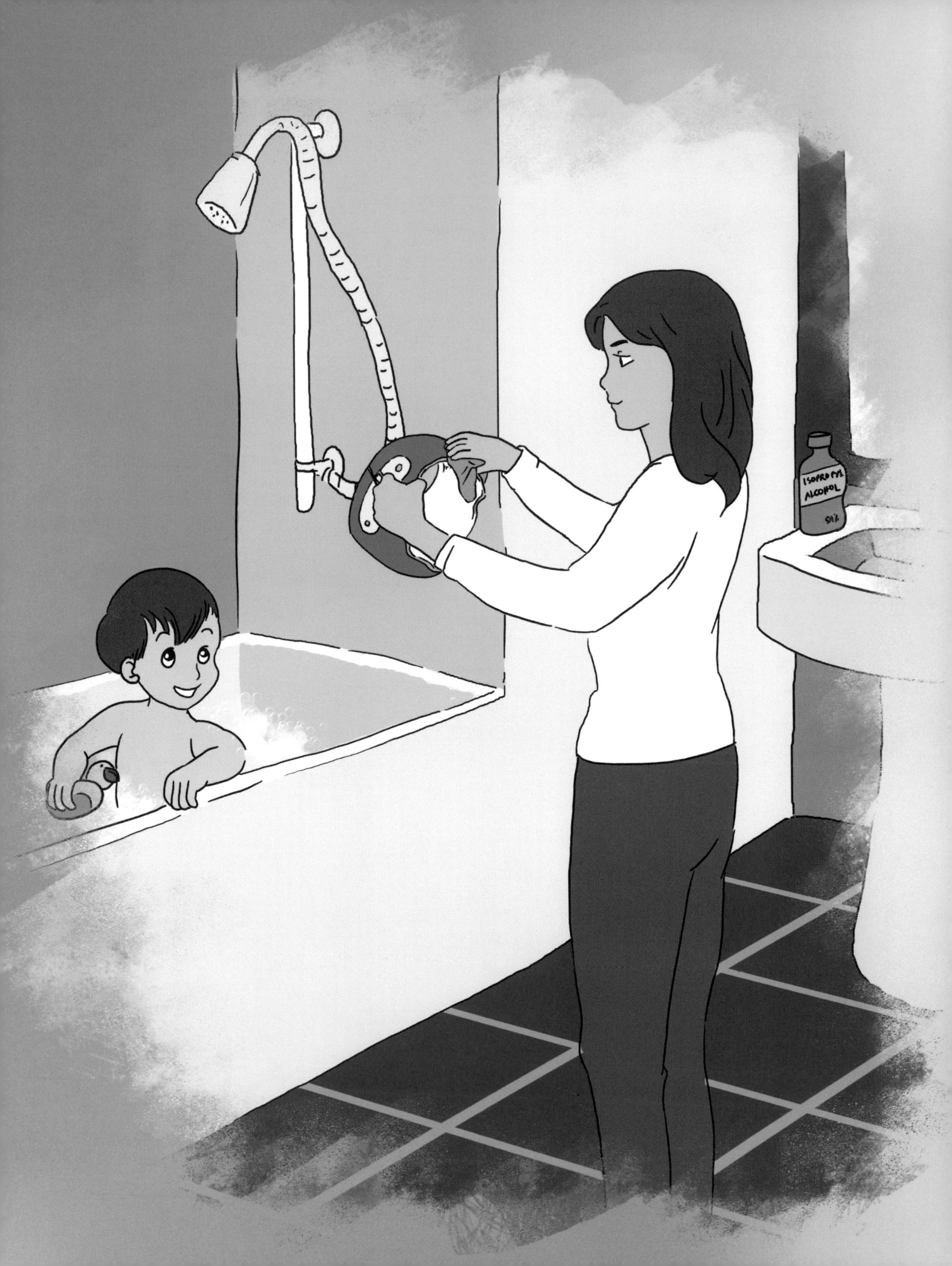
ISOPROPYL
ALCOHOL
91%

"Did I ever take it off?"

"Yes, for one hour each day, you could take it off. We always took it off during your bath time. This was our favorite time of the day."

"Why?" Miller asked.

"Because we could kiss your head over and over," said Mama as she leaned in and kissed his head.

GRATS!
CON
CONGRATS!
"HELMET"
GRADUATE

"Mama, did I wear that helmet for years?"

Mama chuckled and said, "No, but you did wear it for several months."
"Then one day, the doctor said you didn't have to wear it anymore because your head was finally round."

"We called it your helmet graduation day. We had a big celebration!"

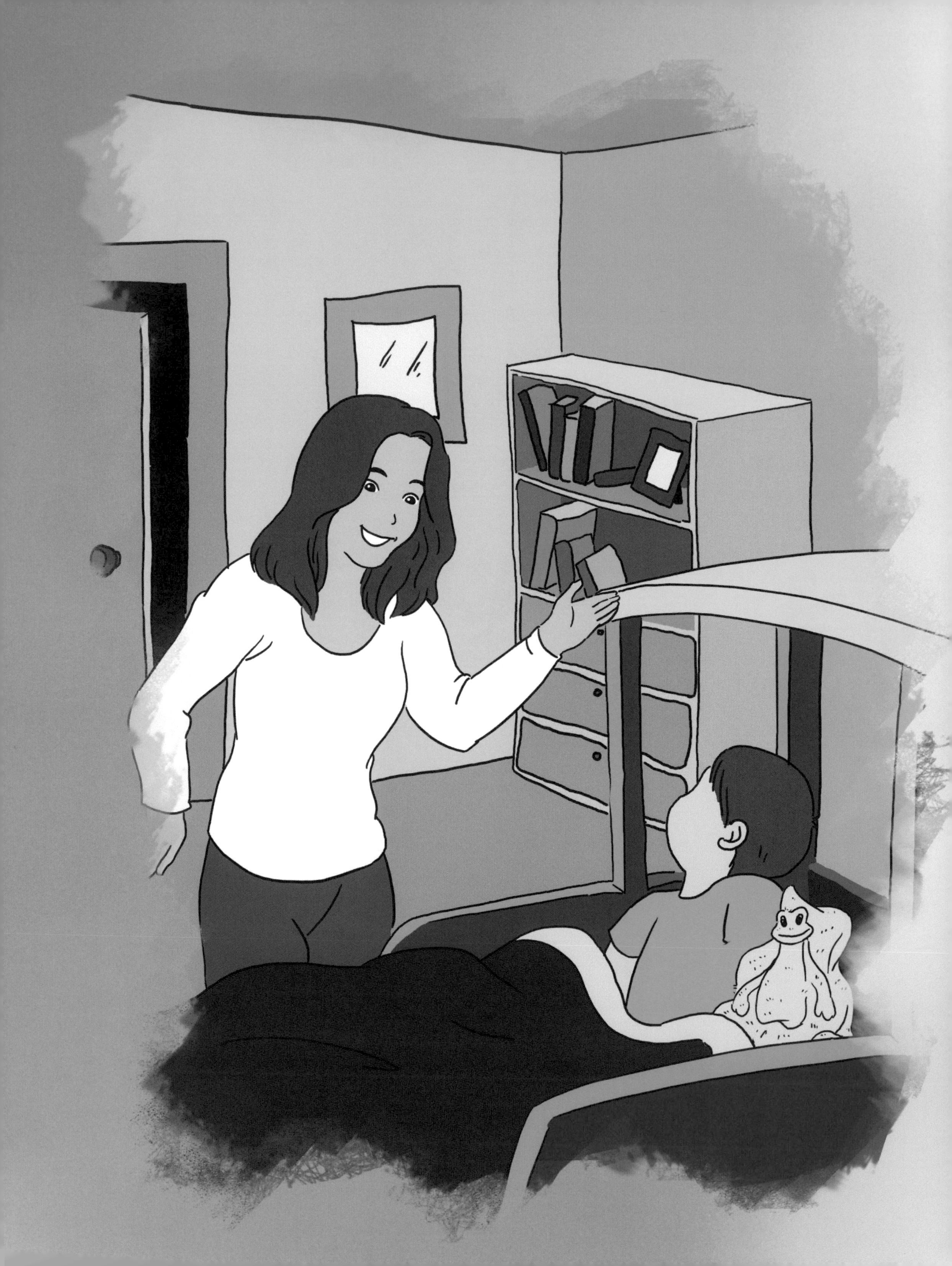

Mama closed the photo album and began tucking Miller into bed.
Miller yawned and said, "I like that story."

"Me too," whispered Mama as she kissed his head and began walking out of the room.

"Mama?"

"Yes?"

"Does God love little boys in little blue helmets?"

Mama smiled and said, "God **especially** loves little boys in little blue helmets."
Miller smiled and closed his eyes.

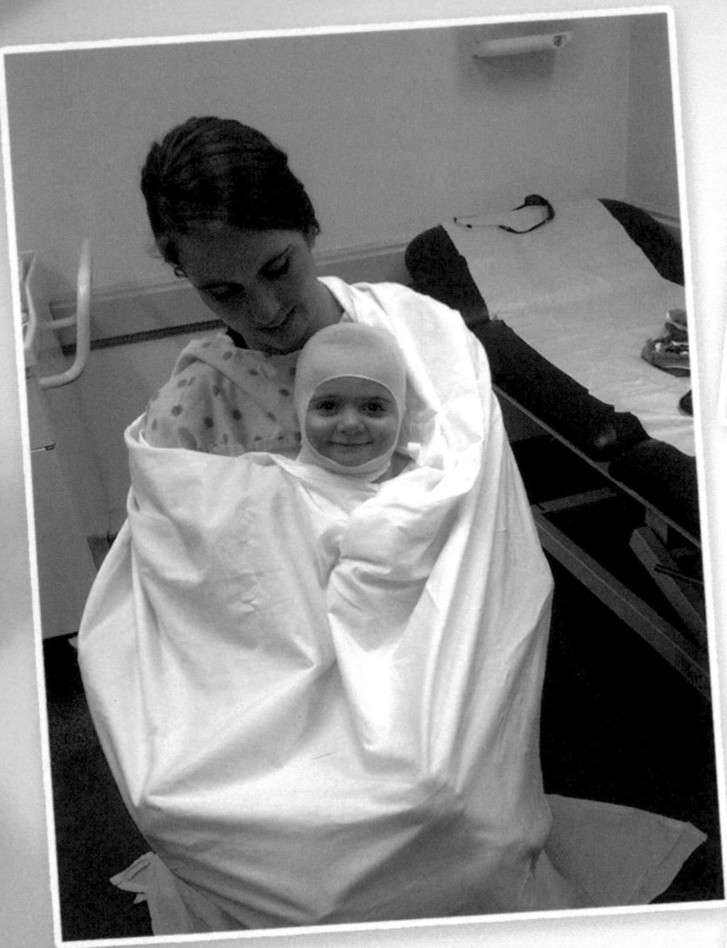

Miller's helmet fitting

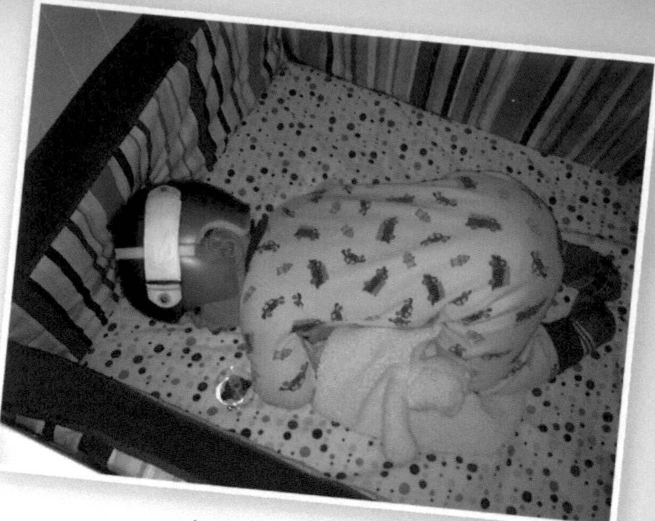

Miller sleeping

Miller at the beach 2012

Miller's helmet graduation day on September 25th, 2012.

(Photo by Amy Beckley Photography)